Library of Congress Cataloging-in-Publication Data

John Paul II, Pope, 1920–
  [selections, English. 2005]
  John Paul II: a Marian treasury / compiled and with an introduction by Marianne Lorraine Trouvé.
    p. cm.
  ISBN 0-8198-3983-3 (hardcover)
  1. Mary, Blessed Virgin, Saint—Meditations. I. Trouvé, Marianne Lorraine. II. Title.
  BX2160.23.J64 2005
  232.91—dc22

                             2004028180

Text reprinted with permission from *L'Osservatore Romano,* English Edition.

Cover Photo: *L'Osservatore Romano* Photo Service / Arturo Mari.

Published by Pauline Books & Media, 50 Saint Pauls Avenue, Boston, MA 02130-3491. Printed in Korea

www.pauline.org

Pauline Books & Media is the publishing house of the Daughters of St. Paul, an international congregation of women religious serving the Church with the communications media.

1 2 3 4 5 6 7 8 9   11 10 09 08 07 06 05

CONTENTS

Introduction   ❀   1

Mary's Faith   ❀   9

Mary, Biblical Woman,
    Mother of the New Creation   ❀   21

Mary's Holiness   ❀   33

Mary, Virgin and Mother   ❀   47

Mary, Mother of Sorrows   ❀   65

Mary's Spiritual Motherhood   ❀   79

Mary and the Eucharist   ❀   95

Mary and the Church   ❀   109

The Rosary and Devotion to Mary   ❀   125

INTRODUCTION

"*Totus tuus!*" Pope John Paul II's motto sums up his profound devotion to Mary. Shortly after his election, he stepped onto the balcony over St. Peter's Square and said he accepted his office "in the spirit of obedience to our Lord Jesus Christ and in total confidence in his Mother, the most holy Madonna." This trust in Mary had struck deep roots in the Pope. As a boy in Poland he learned traditional devotions to Mary and grew to love the "Black Madonna," a copy of which hung in his parish church at Wadowice. His father often brought him on pilgrimage to the Marian shrine at Kalwaria. A significant point came for young Karol when he learned about true devotion to Mary as taught by St. Louis de Montfort:

> When I was working as a clandestine seminarian at the Solvay factory in Kraków, my spiritual director advised me to meditate on the *True Devotion to the Blessed Virgin*. Many times and with great spiritual profit I read and reread this precious little ascetical book with the blue, soda-stained cover.

From that time on, for Karol Wojtyla, Mary has always been a companion and friend.

This love for Mary shines through the impressive body of writings he has given to the Church. His major Marian documents include the encyclical *Mother of the Redeemer (Redemptoris Mater)*, and the apostolic letters *On the Dignity and Vocation of Women (Mulieris Dignitatem)* and *On the Most Holy Rosary (Rosarium Virginis Mariae)*. In fact, he has mentioned Mary in virtually every major document he has written.

While this vast body of material makes it challenging to select certain quotations and exclude others, those included here offer readers a good overview of his Marian thought. Two key principles underlie the Pope's teaching. First, he has promoted Marian devotion in harmony with the teachings of Vatican II. Second, he has spoken about Mary in the context of his personalist approach to theology.

Before becoming Pope, Karol Wojtyla was a professional philosopher who taught at the University of Lublin. There, he and several other philosophers developed a school of thought known as Lublin Thomism. They used insights from St. Thomas Aquinas while developing a moral philosophy that emphasized the dignity of the human person. Among its important concepts are freedom, love, and respect for persons. Called to live in communion with one another, human persons are made in the image of God because that communion reflects the love in the Trinity. Due to its emphasis on what it means to be a person, Wojtyla's approach has been called "personalistic."

But his purpose in this study was not simply academic. As a priest and bishop, he applied such concepts in a pastoral way to help people facing the major questions of human life about love, marriage, and family. Later, when he became Pope, he drew on this background to present the Church's teaching on marriage in a personalistic way that could speak to modern people. This was the basis for John Paul II's greatest contribution as Pope, his theology of the body. The Incarnation gave the human body a central place in Christian revelation. In a series of general audiences, John Paul fully developed this topic, distilling in these talks a lifetime of reflection on the human person.

Although the theology of the body has primarily been applied to the areas of marriage and sexual morality, the Pope has fruitfully applied many of its concepts to Mary. For example, John Paul II speaks of Mary as the biblical exemplar of the "woman," virgin, mother, and spouse, presenting her as the human person who best reflects the image of God. Through her gift of self, Mary expresses what the Pope calls the "law of the gift": that we find fulfillment and happiness to the extent we make a gift of ourselves to God and others. Because the Word took on flesh through Mary, she speaks to us of what it means to live as embodied beings.

Viewing Mary through the personalism of John Paul II, a number of important themes stand out. Although this volume groups together major strands, they are not rigorously divided in the Pope's writings. He writes in a reflective and fluid way, viewing his subject from various aspects. However, one theme stands out as an overarching, unifying concept: *Mary's faith*. John Paul II has written so extensively about Mary's faith that this concept undergirds his entire Marian thought.

Because of her faith, Mary is the *"biblical woman"* who stands at the center of God's plan of salvation. John Paul II sees Mary as having a certain cosmic dimension in the history of God's dealings with the human race. He identifies her not only with the woman of Genesis 3:15 (the *Proto-Evangelium*), whose son will crush the head of the serpent, but also with the woman clothed with the sun in Revelation 12. He uses the well-known parallel between Eve and Mary, but develops it in a unique way. Eve is the witness to the goodness of God's plan of creation, and Mary is the witness to the *new creation*, the redemption. John Paul II also develops a unique parallel between Abraham and Mary. Just as Abraham's faith was the beginning of the covenant God made with Israel, Mary's faith at the Annunciation is the beginning of the new covenant. This sheds light on Mary's role in the whole sweep of salvation history.

This special role calls for a unique *holiness*, which is why God gifted her with the grace of the Immaculate Conception. During her life Mary freely cooperated with grace and became the first disciple of Christ. She exercised faith especially by believing that she would become the *Virgin Mother of God*. Her virginity bears witness to the nuptial meaning of the body. "Mary accepted her election as Mother of the Son of God, guided by spousal love, the love which totally 'consecrates' a human being to God. By virtue of this love, Mary wished to be always and in all things 'given to God,' living in virginity" *(Mother of the Redeemer,* 39).

Mary's divine motherhood is a gift she made of herself to God. "From the outset she accepted and understood her own motherhood as a total *gift of self,* a gift of her person to the service of the saving plans of the Most High" *(Mother of the Redeemer,* 39).

As Mother of God, Mary's supreme act of obedience and faith came on Calvary, when as *Mother of Sorrows,* she became *Mother of the Church.* In this role of *spiritual mother* she was assumed into glory and continually intercedes for us in heaven. John Paul II sees Mary not only as our intercessor, but as our teacher, the one who can best instruct us in the ways of her son, Jesus Christ. He develops this theme of going to the "school of Mary," especially in his encyclical *On the Eucharist in Its Relationship to the Church* and in the letter *On the Most Holy Rosary.* In these two documents he stresses an important aspect of Marian spirituality: Mary's relationship to the Eucharist. This too hinges on the key role of Mary's faith. Since the Eucharist, above all, is the mystery of faith, Mary can help us grow in our Eucharistic faith.

Finally, because John Paul II has promoted the Rosary so tirelessly, the book ends with some of his personal thoughts on this devotion, to which he added the

Mysteries of Light. As he has said, "How many graces have I received in these years from the Blessed Virgin through the Rosary: *Magnificat anima mea Dominum!* I wish to lift up my thanks to the Lord in the words of his Most Holy Mother, under whose protection I have placed my Petrine ministry: *Totus Tuus!*"

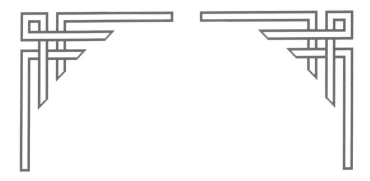

Mary's Faith

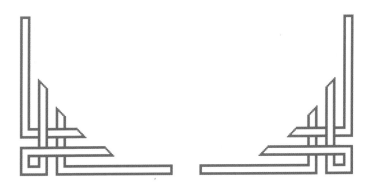

In the expression "Blessed is she who believed," we can rightly find *a kind of "key"* which unlocks for us the innermost reality of Mary, whom the angel hailed as "full of grace." If as "full of grace" she has been eternally present in *the mystery of Christ*, through faith she became a sharer in that mystery in every extension of her earthly journey. 🌸

Mary's docility to the divine will was linked to her faith. Believing in God's word, she could accept it fully in her life and, showing herself receptive to God's sovereign plan, she accepted all that was asked of her from on high. Our Lady's presence in the Church thus encourages Christians to listen to the word of the Lord every day, to understand his loving plan in various daily events, and to cooperate faithfully in bringing it about. 🕸

Once, Abraham believed in God and answered his call, thus inaugurating the great heritage of revealed faith. Now, at the moment of the Annunciation, Mary believes in the words of the divine messenger and inaugurates a new heritage of faith in which the old heritage is taken up and brought to fulfillment. The new heritage of faith, the new and eternal heritage of the Paschal Mystery, the heritage of the crucified and risen Christ, reveals new depths of faith. ❧

uilt by Christ upon the Apostles, the Church became fully aware of the mighty works of God on the day of Pentecost. From that moment there also begins that journey of faith, the Church's pilgrimage through the history of individuals and peoples. We know that at the beginning of this journey Mary is present. We see her in the midst of the Apostles in the Upper Room, "prayerfully imploring the gift of the Spirit." In a sense her journey of faith is longer. The Holy Spirit had already come down upon her, and she became his faithful spouse at the Annunciation, welcoming the Word of the true God. 🌸

Mary has gone before us on the way of faith: believing the angel's message, she was the first to welcome the mystery of the Incarnation and did so perfectly.... Hers was a daring faith. At the Annunciation she believed what was humanly impossible, and at Cana she urged Jesus to work his first miracle, pressing him to manifest his messianic powers. Mary teaches Christians to live their faith as a demanding and engaging journey, which, in every age and situation of life, requires courage and constant perseverance. 🌸

Mary teaches the community of believers to look to the future with total abandonment to God. In the Virgin's personal experience, hope is enriched with ever new reasons. Since the Annunciation, Mary concentrates the expectations of ancient Israel on the Son of God, incarnate in her virginal womb. Her hope was strengthened during the successive stages of Jesus' hidden life in Nazareth and his public ministry. Her great faith in the word of Christ, who had announced his resurrection on the third day, prevented her from wavering, even when faced with the drama of the cross. 🌸

Through her response of faith, Mary exercises her free will and thus fully shares with her personal and feminine "I" in the event of the Incarnation. With her *"fiat," Mary becomes the authentic subject* of that union with God which was realized in the mystery of the Incarnation of the Word, who is of one substance with the Father. All of God's action in human history at all times respects the free will of the human "I." And such was the case with the Annunciation at Nazareth.

ary's faith can also be *compared to that of Abraham*, whom St. Paul calls "our father in faith" (cf. Rom 4:12).... Abraham's faith constitutes the beginning of the old covenant; Mary's faith at the Annunciation inaugurates the new covenant. Just as Abraham *in hope believed against hope*, that he should become the father of many nations" (cf. Rom 4:18), so Mary, at the Annunciation, having professed her virginity...*believed* that through the power of the Most High, by the power of the Holy Spirit, she would become the Mother of God's Son in accordance with the angel's revelation.

ndeed, at the Annunciation Mary entrusted herself to God completely, with the "full submission of intellect and will," manifesting "the obedience of faith" to him who spoke to her through his messenger *(Dei Verbum,* 5). She responded, therefore, *with all her human and feminine "I,"* and this response of faith included both perfect cooperation with "the grace of God that precedes and assists" and perfect openness to the action of the Holy Spirit, who "constantly brings faith to completion by his gifts" *(Lumen Gentium,* 56) . 🌸

o make his covenant with humanity, [God] addressed himself only to men: *Noah, Abraham, and Moses.* At the beginning of the new covenant, which is to be eternal and irrevocable, there is a woman: the Virgin of Nazareth. It is a *sign* that points to the fact that "in Jesus Christ" *"there is neither male nor female"* (Gal 3:28). In Christ the mutual opposition between man and woman—which is the inheritance of original sin—is essentially overcome. "For you are all *one* in Jesus Christ," Saint Paul will write (Gal 3:28).

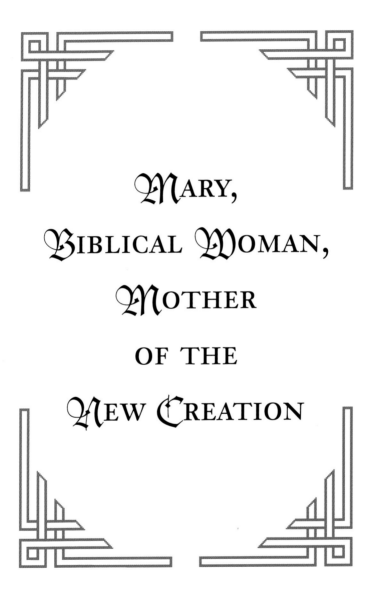

Mary,
Biblical Woman,
Mother
of the
New Creation

She who, as the one "full of grace" was brought into the mystery of Christ in order to be his Mother and thus the Holy Mother of God, through the Church remains in that mystery as "the woman" spoken of by the Book of Genesis (3:15) at the beginning and by the Apocalypse (12:1) at the end of the history of salvation.

he biblical exemplar of the "woman" finds its culmination *in the motherhood of the Mother of God.* The struggle with evil and the Evil One marks the biblical exemplar of the "woman" from the beginning to the end of history. Mary, Mother of the Incarnate Word, is placed at the very center of that enmity— that struggle which accompanies the history of humanity on earth and the history of salvation itself.

*I*n Mary shines forth God's sublime and surprising tenderness for the entire human race: in her, humanity regains its former beauty and the divine plan is revealed to be stronger than evil, capable of offering ever new possibilities of life and salvation. What great horizons are opened by this mystery! To the women of our time, who search—sometimes intensely—for their authentic dignity, she who is "all beautiful" shows the great possibilities of the feminine genius when it is imbued with grace.

Mary's presence in the midst of Israel—a presence so discreet as to pass almost unnoticed by the eyes of her contemporaries—shone very clearly before the Eternal One, who had associated this hidden "daughter of Zion" with the plan of salvation embracing the whole history of humanity.

At the dawn of the New Testament, the gratuitousness of God's mercy reaches the highest degree in Mary. In her, God's predilection, shown to the Chosen People and in particular to the humble and the poor, reaches its culmination. Nourished by the Word of the Lord and the experience of the saints, the Church urges believers to keep their gaze fixed on the Mother of the Redeemer and to consider themselves, like her, loved by God.

he most Blessed Virgin is she who, by the overshadowing of the power of the Trinity, was the creature most closely associated with the work of salvation. The Incarnation of the Word took place beneath her heart, by the power of the Holy Spirit. In her there dawned the new humanity which with Christ was presented in the world in order to bring to completion the original plan of the covenant with God, broken by the disobedience of the first man. 🦋

In the *Magnificat* the Church sees uprooted that sin which is found at the outset of the earthly history of man and woman, the sin of disbelief and of "little faith" in God. In contrast with the "suspicion" which the "father of lies" sowed in the heart of Eve, the first woman, Mary, whom tradition is wont to call the "new Eve" and the true "Mother of the living," boldly proclaims the undimmed truth about God. ❧

In the tradition of faith and of Christian reflection throughout the ages, *the coupling Adam-Christ* is often linked with that of *Eve-Mary*. If Mary is described also as the "new Eve," what are the meanings of this analogy? Certainly there are many. Particularly noteworthy is the meaning which sees Mary as the full revelation of all that is included in the biblical word "woman": a revelation commensurate with the mystery of the redemption.

ve, as "the mother of all the living" (Gen 3:20), is *the witness to the biblical "beginning,"* which contains the truth about the creation of man made in the image and likeness of God and the truth about original sin. *Mary is the witness to the new "beginning"* and the "new creation" (cf. 2 Cor 5:17), since she herself, as the first of the redeemed in salvation history, is "a new creation": she is "full of grace." It is difficult to grasp why the words of the Proto-evangelium place such strong emphasis on the "woman," if it is not admitted that *in her the new and definitive Covenant* of God with humanity *has its beginning,* the *Covenant* in the redeeming blood of Christ. 🕸

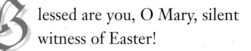lessed are you, O Mary, silent witness of Easter!

You, O Mother of the Crucified One now risen,

who at the hour of pain and death

kept the flame of hope burning,

teach us also to be, among the incongruities of passing time,

convinced and joyful witnesses of life and love

brought to the world by the Risen Redeemer. 🌸

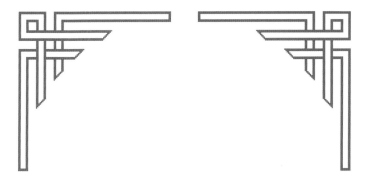

Mary's

Holiness

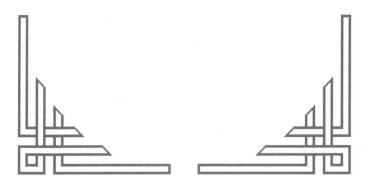

ary belonged always and completely to the Lord, and no imperfection harmed her perfect harmony with God. Her earthly life was marked by a constant, sublime growth in faith, hope, and charity. For believers, Mary is the radiant sign of divine Mercy and the sure guide to the loftiest heights of holiness and Gospel perfection.

It is true that feminine perfection, as it was fully realized in Mary, can at first sight seem to be an exceptional case and impossible to imitate, a model too lofty for imitation. However, far from being a restraint on the way of following the Lord, Mary's exalted holiness is, on the contrary, destined in God's plan to encourage all Christians to open themselves to the sanctifying power of the grace of God, for whom nothing is impossible. ❦

Mary's example enables the Church better to appreciate the value of silence. Mary's silence is not only moderation in speech, but it is especially a wise capacity for remembering and embracing in a single gaze of faith the mystery of the Word made man and the events of his earthly life. It is this silence as acceptance of the Word, this ability to meditate on the mystery of Christ, that Mary passes on to believers. In a noisy world filled with messages of all kinds, her witness enables us to appreciate a spiritually rich silence and fosters a contemplative spirit.

*L*et us look to Mary, whose discreet and holy life is a model of deep unity between interior and exterior efforts. Even in the most complex and painful circumstances, she gave the example of a life totally in harmony and trustingly abandoned to God's will. May the Virgin, Mirror of perfection, obtain for every believer the courage and hope that are indispensable for setting off resolutely on a path of conversion.

Sometimes it is objected that devotion to our Lady, especially popular devotion, risks detracting attention from the center of the faith, which is Jesus, who died and is risen. But this is not so. Through Mary, we come to her Son more easily. Mary is held up as a model for the believer and for the whole Church called to respond to the Lord with her own "yes."

Mary Immaculate is the sign of God's fidelity, which does not yield in the face of human sin. Her fullness of grace also reminds us of the immense possibility for goodness, beauty, greatness, and joy which are within reach of human beings when they let themselves be guided by God's will and reject sin. In the light of her whom the Lord gives us as "our advocate of grace and pattern of holiness," we learn to flee sin always. 🐚

She who at the Annunciation called herself the "handmaid of the Lord" remained throughout her earthly life faithful to what this name expresses. In this she confirmed that she was a true "disciple" of Christ, who strongly emphasized that his mission was one of service. In this way Mary became the first of those who, "serving Christ also in others, with humility and patience lead their brothers and sisters to that King whom to serve is to reign," and she fully obtained that "state of royal freedom" proper to Christ's disciples: to serve means to reign! 🌸

ary was wholly dedicated to serving her Son for years and years. She helped him to grow up and prepare himself for his mission at home and in the carpenter's workshop in Nazareth. At Cana, she asked him to reveal his power as Savior and obtained his first miracle for a couple in difficulty; she has shown us the way of perfect docility to Christ, saying: "Do whatever he tells you" (Jn 2:5).

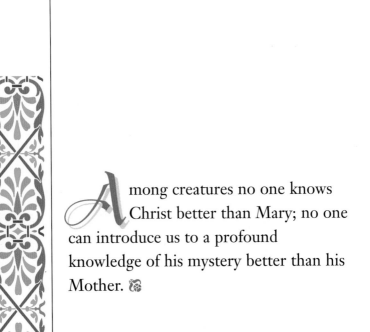

mong creatures no one knows Christ better than Mary; no one can introduce us to a profound knowledge of his mystery better than his Mother.

Mary lived with her eyes fixed on Christ, treasuring his every word: "She kept all these things, pondering them in her heart" (Lk 2:19; cf. 2:51). The memories of Jesus, impressed upon her heart, were always with her, leading her to reflect on the various moments of her life at her Son's side. In a way, those memories were to be the "rosary" which she recited uninterruptedly throughout her earthly life. 🌸

The luminous and holy figure of the Lord's Mother shows how only by self-giving and self-forgetfulness toward others is it possible to attain authentic fulfillment of the divine plan for one's own life. Mary's presence encourages sentiments of mercy and solidarity...and arouses a desire to alleviate the pain of those who suffer: the poor, the sick, and all in need of help. 🏵

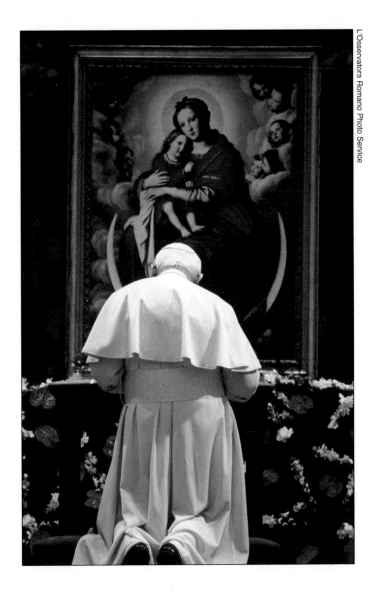

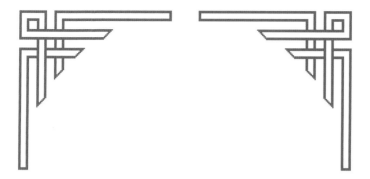

MARY,

VIRGIN AND

MOTHER

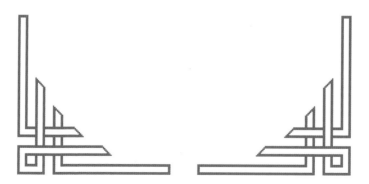

Mary was called to believe in a virginal motherhood.... Mary was asked to assent to a truth never expressed before. She accepted it with a simple yet daring heart. With the question: "How can this be?" she expressed her faith in the divine power to make virginity compatible with her exceptional and unique motherhood.

Asserting Mary's virginity must be done in such a way that one does not appear in any way, directly or indirectly, to lessen the value and dignity of marriage, willed by God.

The words, "Behold, I am the handmaid of the Lord," express the fact that from the outset she accepted and understood her own motherhood as a total gift of self, a gift of her person to the service of the saving plans of the Most High. And to the very end she lived her entire maternal sharing in the life of Jesus Christ, her Son, in a way that matched her vocation to virginity. 🕮

hen theological reflection becomes a moment of doxology and *latria*, the mystery of Mary's virginity is disclosed, allowing one to catch a glimpse of other aspects and other depths. For example...one discerns a particularly important relationship between the beginning and the end of Christ's earthly life, that is, between his virginal conception and his resurrection from the dead, two truths which are closely connected with faith in Jesus' divinity.

ary maintained her virginal "I have no husband" and at the same time became a Mother. Virginity and motherhood co-exist in her: they do not mutually exclude each other or place limits on each other. Indeed, the person of the Mother of God helps everyone—especially women—to see how these two dimensions, these two paths in the vocation of women as persons, explain and complete each other.

hen Mary responds to the words of the heavenly messenger with her *"fiat,"* she who is "full of grace" feels the need to express her personal relationship to the gift that has been revealed to her, saying: *"Behold, I am the handmaid of the Lord"* (Lk 1:38).

We can say that the mystery of the redemption took shape beneath the heart of the Virgin of Nazareth when she pronounced her *"fiat."* From then on, under the special influence of the Holy Spirit, this heart, the heart of both a virgin and a mother, has always followed the work of her Son and has gone out to all those whom Christ has embraced and continues to embrace with inexhaustible love. For that reason her heart must also have the inexhaustibility of a mother.

In [Mary] and through her, [merciful] love continues to be revealed in the history of the Church and of humanity. This revelation is especially fruitful, because in the Mother of God, it is based upon the unique tact of her maternal heart, on her particular sensitivity, on her particular fitness to reach all those who most easily accept the merciful love of a mother. This is one of the great life-giving mysteries of Christianity, a mystery intimately connected with the mystery of the Incarnation.

"Queen of Heaven, rejoice!" Words that express the maternal joy of the Church, who exults together with the Mother of her Lord with the same joy, the joy of life, that is revealed in the resurrection and that lasts forever in God. There is a deep link between the image of the Mother who gives birth to the child and that of the Good Shepherd who lays down his life for his sheep. Those who give life in love receive it anew.

Mary...is the one who has the deepest knowledge of the mystery of God's mercy. She knows its price, she knows how great it is. In this sense, we call her the Mother of Mercy, our Lady of Mercy, or Mother of Divine Mercy; in each one of these titles there is a deep theological meaning, for they express the special preparation of her soul, of her whole personality.

Mary's will to preserve her virginity is surprising in a context where this ideal was not widespread. Her decision was the fruit of a special grace of the Holy Spirit, who opened her heart to the desire to offer herself totally, body and soul, to God, thus bringing about in the loftiest and humanly inconceivable way Israel's vocation to a spousal relationship with God, to belonging totally and exclusively to him as the People of God. ❧

The angel, who proposed that she become a mother, is reminded by Mary of her intention to remain a virgin. Believing that the announcement could be fulfilled, she questions the divine messenger only about the manner of its accomplishment, in order better to fulfill God's will, to which she intends to submit with total readiness. "She sought the manner; she did not doubt God's omnipotence," Saint Augustine remarks. Mary is asked to assent to a truth never expressed before. She accepts it with a simple yet daring heart. 🐝

God treated Mary as a free and responsible person and did not bring about the Incarnation of his Son until after he had obtained her consent.

The event at Nazareth highlights a form of union with the living God which can *only belong to the "woman,"* Mary: *the union between mother and son.* The Virgin of Nazareth truly becomes the Mother of God.

In a highly significant way, the most ancient prayer to Mary ("We fly to your protection...") contains the invocation: "*Theotokos*, Mother of God." This title did not originally come from the reflection of theologians but from an intuition of faith of the Christian people. Those who acknowledge Jesus as God address Mary as the Mother of God and hope to obtain her powerful aid in the trials of life. 🌸

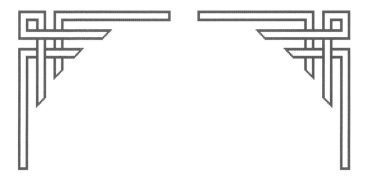

Mary,
Mother of
Sorrows

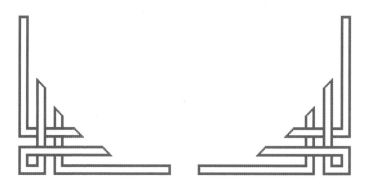

O Mary,
Mother of Mercy,
watch over all people,
that the cross of Christ
may not be emptied of its power,
that man may not stray
from the path of the good
or become blind to sin,
but may put his hope ever more fully
in God
who is "rich in mercy" (Eph 2:4).
May he carry out the good works
prepared by God beforehand (cf. Eph
2:10) and so live completely
"for the praise of his glory" (Eph 1:12).

As a witness to her Son's passion by her presence, and as a sharer in it by her compassion, Mary offered a unique contribution to the Gospel of suffering.... She truly has a special title to be able to claim that she "completes in her flesh"—as already in her heart—"what is lacking in Christ's afflictions" (cf. Col 1:24). 🦋

Simeon's words ["A sword shall pierce your heart"] seem like a *second Annunciation to Mary*, for they tell her of the actual historical situation in which the Son is to accomplish his mission, namely, in misunderstanding and sorrow.

Through this faith Mary is perfectly united with Christ in his self-emptying.... At the foot of the cross Mary shares through faith in the shocking mystery of this self-emptying. This is perhaps the deepest *"kenosis" of faith* in human history. Through faith the Mother shares in the death of her Son, in his redeeming death. 🌸

This "new motherhood of Mary," generated by faith, is *the fruit of the "new" love* which came to definitive maturity in her at the foot of the cross, through her sharing in the redemptive love of her Son.

On seeing his mother beside the cross, Jesus recalled the memories of Nazareth, Cana, and Jerusalem. Perhaps he reviewed in memory the moments of Joseph's death, and then of his own separation from her.... For her part, Mary considered all the things which for years and years "she had kept in her heart" (cf. Lk 2:19, 51). Then more than ever, she understood them in connection with the cross. Sorrow and faith were united in her heart. And then, at a certain point, she became aware that Jesus was looking at her and speaking to her from the cross. 🏵

The Gospel stories never mention the tears of our Lady.... We do not know anything even about her tears of joy when Jesus rose again. Even if Sacred Scripture makes no reference to this fact, the intuition of faith does however speak in its favor. Mary who weeps with sadness or joy is the expression of the Church, which rejoices on Christmas night, suffers on Good Friday at the foot of the cross, and again rejoices at the dawn of the resurrection.

We recall Mary beside her Son on Calvary. There was the presence of a woman—already widowed for years, as everything suggests—who was about to lose her Son also. Every fiber of her being was shaken by what she felt and offered now, beside the cross of execution. How could one prevent her from suffering and weeping? Christian tradition has perceived the dramatic experience of that woman full of dignity and decorum, but with a broken heart, and has paused to contemplate her while participating intimately in her sorrow. 🌺

ary's presence beside the cross indicates her commitment of total sharing in her Son's redemptive sacrifice. Mary had willed to participate to the very depth in the sufferings of Jesus because she did not reject the sword foretold to her by Simeon. Instead, she accepted with Christ the mysterious plan of the Father. She was the first to partake in that sacrifice, and she would forever remain the perfect model of all those who would agree to associate themselves unreservedly with the redemptive offering.

ary is...the one who obtained mercy in a particular and exceptional way, as no other person has. At the same time, still in an exceptional way, she made possible with the sacrifice of her heart her own sharing in revealing God's mercy. This sacrifice is intimately linked with the cross of her Son, at the foot of which she was to stand on Calvary.

No one has experienced, to the same degree as the Mother of the Crucified One, the mystery of the cross, the overwhelming encounter of divine transcendent justice with love: that "kiss" given by mercy to justice. No one has received into his heart, as much as Mary did, that mystery, that truly divine dimension of the redemption effected on Calvary by means of the death of the Son, together with the sacrifice of her maternal heart, together with her definitive *"fiat."* ❧

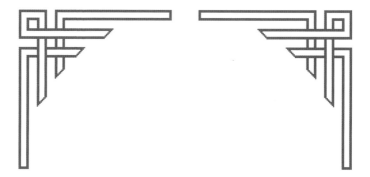

MARY'S SPIRITUAL MOTHERHOOD

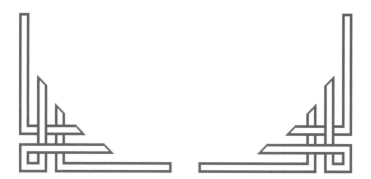

Do not fear to take Mary as your mother on the journey of life! May Mary be a model for you of how to follow Jesus. Do not be afraid of confiding in her, of entrusting to her maternal hands every problem, every anxiety, every expectation, and every project. Above all, trust her with the project that concerns your whole life: your vocation, in the sincere gift of what you are, for your own self-fulfillment.

ary's motherhood in our regard does not only consist of an affective bond; because of her merits and her intercession she contributes effectively to our spiritual birth and to the development of the life of grace within us. This is why Mary is called "Mother of Grace" and "Mother of Life." Mary is our Mother: this consoling truth, offered to us ever more clearly and profoundly by the love and faith of the Church, has sustained and sustains the spiritual life of us all and encourages us, even in suffering, to have faith and hope.

Mary is the Mother who intercedes for all: for souls thirsting for God and for those who are groping in the darkness of doubt and disbelief, for those who are suffering in body or tired in spirit, for those who yield to the attraction of sin and for those who are struggling to escape its clutches. Her motherly concern overlooks no one.

In the midst of struggles, we invite you to lift your gaze to the Blessed Virgin Mary whom Jesus has given us as our Mother. She is present as a Mother and shares in the many complicated problems which today beset the lives of individuals, families, and nations. She is present to the Christian people and helps it in the constant struggle between good and evil, to ensure that it "does not fall," or, if it has fallen, that it "rises again." We implore her to assist us and to show herself a Mother to us.

*L*et us seek to enter into communion with the Immaculate Heart of the Mother of Jesus, where the pain of the Son for the world's salvation was reflected in a unique and incomparable way. Let us receive Mary, designated the spiritual mother of his disciples by the dying Christ, and entrust ourselves to her so as to be faithful to God on the journey from Baptism to glory. 🌼

y taking Mary into his own home, John showed her his filial affection.... John's action was the execution of Jesus' testament in regard to Mary. But it had a symbolic value for each one of Christ's disciples, who are asked to make room for Mary in their lives, to take her into their own homes. By virtue of these words of the dying Christ, every Christian life must offer a space to Mary and provide for her presence. 🕸

ary, who from the beginning had given herself without reserve to the person and work of her Son, could not but pour out upon the Church, from the very beginning, her maternal self-giving. After her Son's departure, her motherhood remains in the Church as maternal mediation: interceding for all her children, the Mother cooperates in the saving work of her Son, the Redeemer of the world. 🏵

May all the Lord's disciples come to appreciate more fully the mystery of Mary's universal motherhood, acknowledging her as their own spiritual Mother and placing their complete trust in her maternal love. ❧

ary's mediation is intimately linked with her motherhood. It possesses a specifically maternal character, which distinguishes it from the mediation of the other creatures who in various and always subordinate ways share in the one mediation of Christ, although her own mediation is also a shared mediation.

From Christ, Mary receives the power to carry out her mission of maternal intercession on behalf of the Church and all humanity. As the Queen who reigns in the glory of God's Kingdom, Mary remains close to us at every step of our earthly pilgrimage, supporting us in our trials and sharing with us the life and love of Jesus her Son. 🕮

Mary's motherhood, which becomes man's inheritance, is a gift: a gift which Christ himself makes personally to every individual. The Redeemer entrusts Mary to John because he entrusts John to Mary. At the foot of the cross there begins that special entrusting of humanity to the Mother of Christ, which in the history of the Church has been practiced and expressed in different ways.

The Marian dimension of the life of a disciple of Christ is expressed in a special way precisely through this filial entrusting to the Mother of Christ, which began with the testament of the Redeemer on Golgotha. Entrusting himself to Mary in a filial manner, the Christian, like the Apostle John, "welcomes" the Mother of Christ "into his own home" and brings her into everything that makes up his inner life, that is to say, into his human and Christian "I": he "took her to his own home."

"Woman, behold your Son!"
(Jn 19:26).
When he entrusted to you the Apostle
John,
and with him the children of the
Church and all people,
Christ did not diminish
but affirmed anew
the role which is his alone as the Savior
of the world.
You are the splendor which in no way
dims the light of Christ,
for you exist in him and through him.
Everything in you is *fiat:* you are the
Immaculate One,
through you there shines the fullness of
grace.

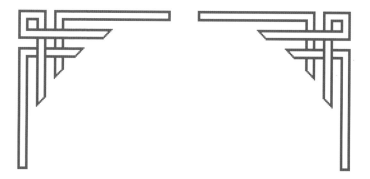

MARY AND
THE EUCHARIST

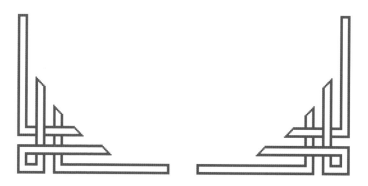

Mary is a "woman of the Eucharist" in her whole life. The Church, which looks to Mary as a model, is also called to imitate her in her relationship with this most holy mystery.

ysterium fidei! If the Eucharist is a mystery of faith which so greatly transcends our understanding as to call for sheer abandonment to the Word of God, then there can be no one like Mary to act as our support and guide in acquiring this disposition.

With the same maternal concern which she showed at the wedding feast of Cana, Mary seems to say to us: "Do not waver; trust in the words of my Son. If he was able to change water into wine, he can also turn bread and wine into his body and blood, and through this mystery bestow on believers the living memorial of his Passover, thus becoming the 'bread of life.'"

ary lived her *Eucharistic faith* even before the institution of the Eucharist, by the very fact that *she offered her virginal womb for the Incarnation of God's Word....* At the Annunciation Mary conceived the Son of God in the physical reality of his body and blood, thus anticipating within herself what to some degree happens sacramentally in every believer who receives, under the signs of bread and wine, the Lord's body and blood. 🏵

There is a profound analogy between the *fiat* which Mary said in reply to the angel, and the *Amen* which every believer says when receiving the body of the Lord. Mary was asked to believe that the One whom she conceived "through the Holy Spirit" was "the Son of God" (Lk 1:30–35). In continuity with the Virgin's faith, in the Eucharistic mystery we are asked to believe that the same Jesus Christ, Son of God and Son of Mary, becomes present in his full humanity and divinity under the signs of bread and wine.

"Blessed is she who believed" (Lk 1:45). Mary also anticipated, in the mystery of the Incarnation, the Church's Eucharistic faith. When, at the Visitation, she bore in her womb the Word made flesh, she became in some way a "tabernacle"—the first "tabernacle" in history—in which the Son of God, still invisible to our human gaze, allowed himself to be adored by Elizabeth, radiating his light as it were through the eyes and the voice of Mary.

ary, throughout her life at Christ's side and not only on Calvary, made her own *the sacrificial dimension of the Eucharist.* When she brought the child Jesus to the Temple in Jerusalem "to present him to the Lord" (Lk 2:22), she heard the aged Simeon announce that the child would be a "sign of contradiction" and that a sword would also pierce her own heart (cf. Lk 2:34–35). The tragedy of her Son's crucifixion was thus foretold, and in some sense Mary's *Stabat Mater* at the foot of the cross was foreshadowed.

In her daily preparation for Calvary, Mary experienced a kind of "anticipated Eucharist"—one might say a "spiritual communion"—of desire and of oblation, which would culminate in her union with her Son in his passion, and then find expression after Easter by her partaking in the Eucharist which the Apostles celebrated as the memorial of that passion.

hat must Mary have felt as she heard from the mouth of Peter, John, James, and the other Apostles the words spoken at the Last Supper: "This is my body which is given for you" (Lk 22:19)? The body given up for us and made present under sacramental signs was the same body which she had conceived in her womb! For Mary, receiving the Eucharist must have somehow meant welcoming once more into her womb that heart which had beat in unison with hers and reliving what she had experienced at the foot of the cross.

"Do this in remembrance of me" (Lk 22:19). In the "memorial" of Calvary all that Christ accomplished by his passion and his death is present. Consequently *all that Christ did with regard to his Mother* for our sake is also present. To her he gave the beloved disciple and, in him, each of us: "Behold, your son!" To each of us he also says: "Behold your mother!" (cf. Jn 19:26–27).

Experiencing the memorial of Christ's death in the Eucharist also means continually receiving this gift. It means accepting—like John—the one who is given to us anew as our Mother. It also means taking on a commitment to be conformed to Christ, putting ourselves at the school of his Mother and allowing her to accompany us. Mary is present, with the Church and as the Mother of the Church, at each of our celebrations of the Eucharist. If the Church and the Eucharist are inseparably united, the same ought to be said of Mary and the Eucharist.

ary, "Eucharistic" Woman who offered your virginal womb for the Incarnation of the Word of God, help us to live the Eucharistic Mystery in the spirit of the *"Magnificat."* May our lives be a never-ending praise of the Almighty who concealed himself beneath the humility of the Eucharistic signs. 🥀

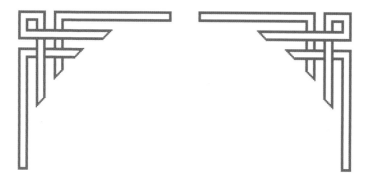

MARY AND
THE CHURCH

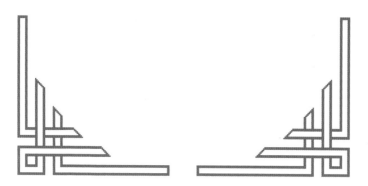

Mary is present in the Church as the Mother of Christ, and at the same time as that Mother whom Christ, in the mystery of the redemption, gave to humanity in the person of the Apostle John. Thus, in her new motherhood in the Spirit, Mary embraces each and everyone in the Church, and embraces each and everyone through the Church. In this sense Mary, Mother of the Church, is also the Church's model.

he Second Vatican Council, confirming the teaching of the whole of tradition, recalled that in the hierarchy of holiness it is *precisely the "woman,"* Mary of Nazareth, who is the "figure" of the Church. She "precedes" everyone on the path to holiness; in her person "the Church has already reached that perfection whereby she exists without spot or wrinkle (cf. Eph 5:27)" *(Lumen Gentium,* 65). In this sense, one can say that the Church is *both* "Marian" and "Apostolic-Petrine."

The Virgin Mary is the archetype of the Church because of the divine maternity; just like Mary, the Church must be, and wishes to be, mother and virgin. The Church lives in this authentic "Marian profile," this "Marian dimension."

It is precisely *in this ecclesial journey or pilgrimage* through space and time, and even more through the history of souls, that *Mary is present*, as the one who is "blessed because she believed," as the one who advanced on the pilgrimage of faith.... Mary, through the same faith which made her blessed, especially from the moment of the Annunciation, is *present* in the Church's mission, *present* in the Church's work of introducing into the world *the kingdom of her Son.*

This heroic *faith* of hers *"precedes"* the apostolic witness of the Church and ever remains in the Church's heart, hidden like a special heritage of God's revelation. All those who from generation to generation accept the apostolic witness of the Church share in that mysterious inheritance, and *in a sense share in Mary's faith*. It is precisely this lively sharing in Mary's faith that determines her special place in the Church's pilgrimage as the new People of God throughout the earth.

The Church...takes up the great challenge contained in these words of the Marian antiphon: "the people who have fallen yet strive to rise again," and she addresses both the Redeemer and his Mother with the plea: "Assist us." For, as this prayer attests, the Church sees the Blessed Mother of God in the saving mystery of Christ and in her own mystery. She sees Mary deeply rooted in humanity's history, in man's eternal vocation according to the providential plan which God has made for him from eternity. 🏵

he Council itself offers us a criterion for discerning authentic Marian doctrine: Mary "occupies a place in the Church which is the highest after Christ and also closest to us." The highest place: we must discover this lofty position granted to Mary in the mystery of salvation. However, it is a question of a vocation totally in relationship to Christ. The place closest to us: our life is profoundly influenced by Mary's example and intercession.... The entire teaching of salvation history invites us to look to the Virgin. 🐚

As a mother, Mary desires the union of all her children. Her presence in the Church is an invitation to preserve the unanimity of heart which reigned in the first community and, consequently, to seek ways of unity and peace among all men and women of good will. In interceding with her Son, Mary asks the grace of unity for all humanity, in view of building a civilization of love, overcoming tendencies to division, temptations to revenge and hatred, and the perverse fascination of violence. 🌸

Mary appears to Christians of all times as the one who feels deep compassion for the sufferings of humanity. This compassion does not consist only in an emotional sympathy, but is expressed in effective and concrete help when confronted with humanity's material and moral misery. In following Mary, the Church is called to take on the same attitude toward all the earth's poor and suffering.

ary's universal mission is exercised in the context of her unique relationship with the Church. With her concern for every Christian, and indeed for every human creature, Mary guides the faith of the Church toward an ever deeper acceptance of God's Word, sustains her hope, enlivens her charity and fraternal communion, and encourages her apostolic dynamism.

The maternal attention of the Lord's Mother to the tears, sorrows, and hardships of the men and women of all ages must spur Christians, particularly at the dawn of the new millennium, to increase the concrete and visible signs of a love that will enable today's humble and suffering people to share in the promises and hopes of the new world which is born from Easter. 🌸

he development of Mariological thought and devotion to the Blessed Virgin down the centuries has contributed to revealing ever better the Church's Marian aspect. Of course, the Blessed Virgin is totally related to Christ, the foundation of faith and ecclesial experience, and she leads to him. That is why, in obedience to Jesus, who reserved a very special role for his Mother in the economy of salvation, Christians have venerated, loved, and prayed to Mary in a most particular and fervent way.

The Church's Marian dimension is an undeniable element in the experience of the Christian people. It is expressed in many ways in the life of believers, testifying to the place Mary holds in their hearts. It is not a superficial sentiment but a deep and conscious emotional bond, rooted in the faith which spurs Christians of the past and present to turn habitually to Mary, to enter into a more intimate communion with Christ.

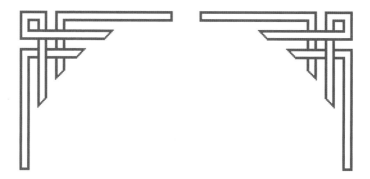

The Rosary
and Devotion
to Mary

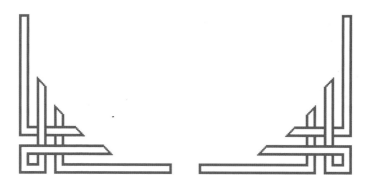

To pray the Rosary is to hand over our burdens to the merciful hearts of Christ and his Mother. 🌸

With the Rosary, the Christian people *sits at the school of Mary* and is led to contemplate the beauty on the face of Christ and to experience the depths of his love. Through the Rosary the faithful receive abundant grace, as though from the very hands of the Mother of the Redeemer.

To recite the Rosary is nothing other than to *contemplate with Mary the face of Christ*.... In contemplating Christ's face we become open to receiving the mystery of Trinitarian life, experiencing ever anew the love of the Father, and delighting in the joy of the Holy Spirit.

The first of the "signs" worked by Jesus—the changing of water into wine at the marriage in Cana—clearly presents Mary in the guise of a teacher, as she urges the servants to do what Jesus commands (cf. Jn 2:5). We can imagine that she would have done likewise for the disciples after Jesus' ascension, when she joined them in awaiting the Holy Spirit.... Contemplating the scenes of the Rosary in union with Mary is a means of learning from her to "read" Christ, to discover his secrets, and to understand his message.

In the spiritual journey of the Rosary, based on the constant contemplation—in Mary's company—of the face of Christ, this demanding ideal of being conformed to him is pursued through an association which could be described in terms of friendship. We are thereby enabled to enter naturally into Christ's life and as it were to share his deepest feelings.

he Rosary mystically transports us to Mary's side as she is busy watching over the human growth of Christ in the home of Nazareth. This enables her to train us and to mold us with the same care, until Christ is "fully formed" in us (cf. Gal 4:19).

Never as in the Rosary do the life of Jesus and that of Mary appear so deeply joined. Mary lives only in Christ and for Christ! ❧

The Rosary is both meditation and supplication. Insistent prayer to the Mother of God is based on confidence that her maternal intercession can obtain all things from the heart of her Son.

The Rosary is at the service of this ideal; it offers the "secret" which leads easily to a profound and inward knowledge of Christ. We might call it *Mary's way*. It is the way of the example of the Virgin of Nazareth, a woman of faith, of silence, of attentive listening. It is also the way of a Marian devotion inspired by knowledge of the inseparable bond between Christ and his Blessed Mother: *the mysteries of Christ* are also in some sense *the mysteries of his Mother*.

It becomes natural to bring to this encounter with the sacred humanity of the Redeemer all the problems, anxieties, labors, and endeavors which go to make up our lives. "Cast your burden on the Lord and he will sustain you" (Ps 55:23). To pray the Rosary is to hand over our burdens to the merciful hearts of Christ and his Mother. 🌸

To understand the Rosary, one has to enter into the psychological dynamic proper to love. One thing is clear: although the repeated *Hail Mary* is addressed directly to Mary, it is to Jesus that the act of love is ultimately directed, with her and through her. The repetition is nourished by the desire to be conformed ever more completely to Christ, the true program of the Christian life. Saint Paul expressed this project with words of fire: "For me to live is Christ and to die is gain" (Phil 1:21).

I look to all of you, brothers and sisters of every state of life, to you, Christian families, to you, the sick and elderly, and to you, young people: *confidently take up the Rosary once again.* Rediscover the Rosary in the light of Scripture, in harmony with the liturgy, and in the context of your daily lives.

oly Virgin, we proclaim blessed the fruit of your womb. Help us to understand his words which are demanding but true, and which for this very reason can inspire genuine joy in hearts. Sorrowful Virgin, grant that we may have the mind of Christ, your Son; help us to follow him up the steep path of Calvary in order to find in the cross the secret of new life, a life no longer subject to death. Glorious Virgin, in times of difficulty, restore our hope that we will meet God in bliss, on that day when "we shall be like him, for we shall see him as he is" (1 Jn 3:2). 🦋

BOOKS & MEDIA

The Daughters of St. Paul operate book and media centers at the following addresses. Visit, call or write the one nearest you today, or find us on the World Wide Web, www.pauline.org

CALIFORNIA

3908 Sepulveda Blvd, Culver City, CA 90230	310-397-8676
5945 Balboa Avenue, San Diego, CA 92111	858-565-9181
46 Geary Street, San Francisco, CA 94108	415-781-5180

FLORIDA

145 S.W. 107th Avenue, Miami, FL 33174	305-559-6715

HAWAII

1143 Bishop Street, Honolulu, HI 96813	808-521-2731
Neighbor Islands call:	800-259-8463

ILLINOIS

172 North Michigan Avenue, Chicago, IL 60601	312-346-4228

LOUISIANA

4403 Veterans Memorial Blvd, Metairie, LA 70006	504-887-7631

MASSACHUSETTS

885 Providence Hwy, Dedham, MA 02026	781-326-5385

MISSOURI

9804 Watson Road, St. Louis, MO 63126	314-965-3512

NEW JERSEY

561 U.S. Route 1, Wick Plaza, Edison, NJ 08817	732-572-1200

NEW YORK

150 East 52nd Street, New York, NY 10022	212-754-1110
78 Fort Place, Staten Island, NY 10301	718-447-5071

PENNSYLVANIA

9171-A Roosevelt Blvd, Philadelphia, PA 19114	215-676-9494

SOUTH CAROLINA

243 King Street, Charleston, SC 29401	843-577-0175

TENNESSEE

4811 Poplar Avenue, Memphis, TN 38117	901-761-2987

TEXAS

114 Main Plaza, San Antonio, TX 78205	210-224-8101

VIRGINIA

1025 King Street, Alexandria, VA 22314	703-549-3806

CANADA

3022 Dufferin Street, Toronto, ON M6B 3T5	416-781-9131